The CRAFTY HANDS *Collection*

Rag Dolls
Salt Dough Models
Simple Projects in Patchwork
Face Painting & Fancy Dress

First published in English in Great Britain
1995 by Aurum Press Ltd,
25 Bedford Avenue, London WC1B 3AT

Translated by Lydia Darbyshire

First published as
Poupées-Câlin, Poupées-Colère
1989 by Éditions Fleurus,
11 rue Duguay-Trouin, 75006 Paris, France

A catalogue record for this book is available from the British Library

ISBN 1 85410 329 6

1 3 5 7 9 10 8 6 4 2
1995 1997 1999 1998 1996

Printed in Italy

RAG DOLLS

Bernadette Theulet-Luzié

Aurum Press

INTRODUCTION

Making a doll for yourself or for someone you love is always a pleasure. Part of the enjoyment comes, of course, from choosing the materials, and deciding on the style and the decorations, but the most enjoyable and challenging part of creating a doll is giving it a character.

This book contains instructions for making a dozen soft dolls. They are all made from stockinette or fine jersey, and they are filled with polyester stuffing or kapok. Practically all of them are made in the same way; there is a simple pattern for the basic body (see pages 6–7), which is then dressed in different ways – as a fairy or a princess, as a footballer or even Superman.

You will find a doll to suit every occasion – an artist to give to a painter, a chef to give to a cook or a hitch-hiker for someone who is going on a journey. Alternatively, of course, you can dress your doll in whatever way you want.

Contents

Note
All the grids are shown half-size.
1 square = 2cm/$^3/_4$in.

4

MAKING THE BODY

Almost all the dolls on the pages that follow are made in exactly the same way. Only the clothes and accessories vary from one doll to another.

The bodies are made from white or flesh-coloured jersey and are stuffed with polyester fibre or kapok. The instructions for the dolls made in a different way – Superman, the Pixie and Little Mischief – explain how the bodies are assembled. The bodies of all the other dolls are made as shown here.

For each doll you will need a piece of jersey about 51 x 24cm/20 x 9½in. Each doll is made from five 'bags': one for the head and body, 24 x 14cm/9½ x 5½in; two for the arms, 11 x 11cm/4½ x 4½in; and two for the legs, 12 x 12cm/ 4¾ x 4¾in. Seam allowances of 5mm/¼in are included in all these dimensions.

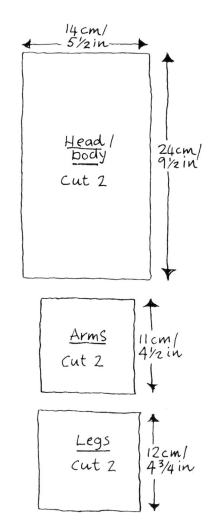

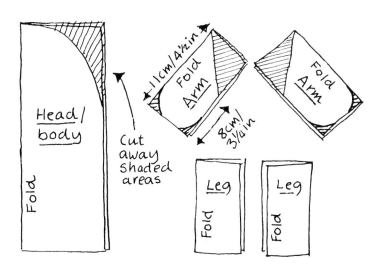

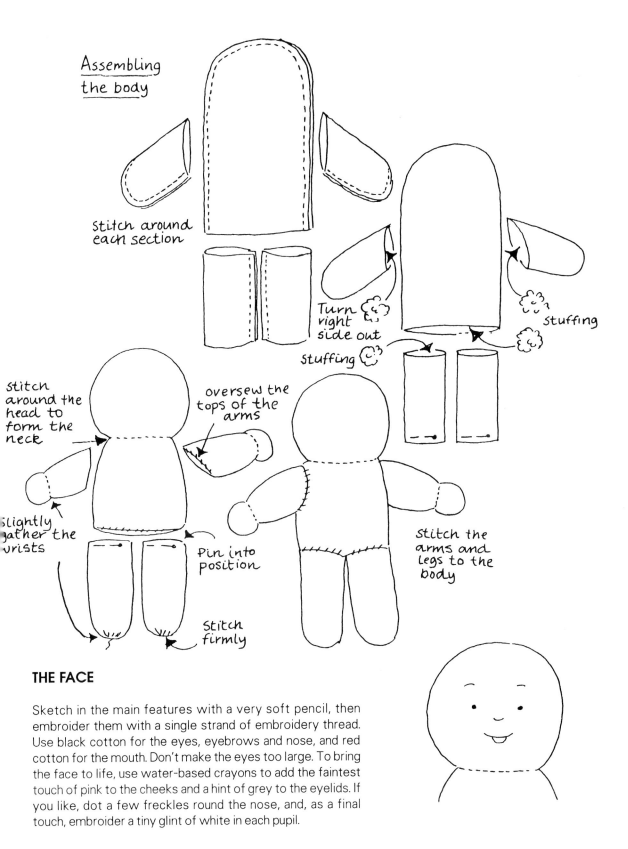

Assembling the body

stitch around each section

Turn right side out

stuffing

stuffing

stitch around the head to form the neck

oversew the tops of the arms

slightly gather the wrists

Pin into position

stitch firmly

stitch the arms and legs to the body

THE FACE

Sketch in the main features with a very soft pencil, then embroider them with a single strand of embroidery thread. Use black cotton for the eyes, eyebrows and nose, and red cotton for the mouth. Don't make the eyes too large. To bring the face to life, use water-based crayons to add the faintest touch of pink to the cheeks and a hint of grey to the eyelids. If you like, dot a few freckles round the nose, and, as a final touch, embroider a tiny glint of white in each pupil.

SHOES AND SOCKS

These instructions for making shoes and socks apply to almost all the dolls, and they can be easily adapted to suit the style of doll you are making.

Copy the outlines onto the fabric of your choice. Depending on the doll, you will need either four soles or two soles and two 'uppers'. Cut them out in pairs, adding a seam allowance of 5mm/¼in. Unless you are using felt, you will need to cut V-shaped notches around the edges.

To make one sock

Stitch, turn right side out

Slip over the leg   Turn down the sock top

To make one shoe

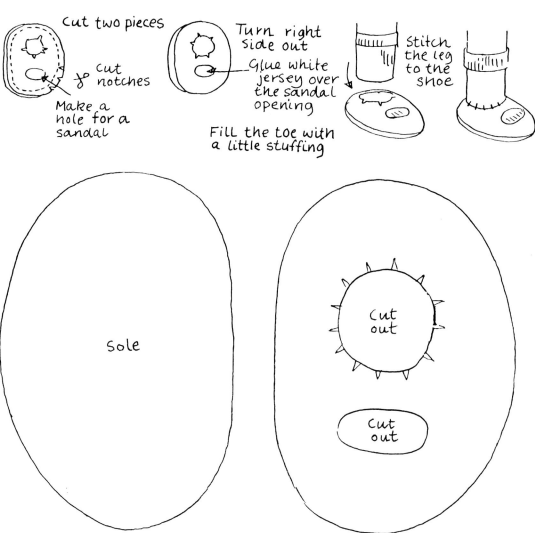

Cut two pieces

Cut notches

Make a hole for a sandal

Turn right side out

Glue white jersey over the sandal opening

Fill the toe with a little stuffing

Stitch the leg to the shoe

Sole

Cut out

Cut out

HAIR

You will need a surprising amount of wool – about a ball or a hank. Choose colours that are as close as possible to natural shades – black is too severe and straw yellow is better than lemony yellow. If you want your doll to have auburn hair, choose brick-red, which looks more subtle than scarlet. Of the dolls in this book, only the witch has got strangely coloured hair – green seemed appropriate.

For long hair you will need to cut pieces 40cm/16in long; for mid-length hair you will need pieces 30cm/12in long; and for short hair, cut pieces 25cm/10in long.

Stitch the lengths into position along a line that will form the parting. When the hair is in place, trim it to length, curl it, ruffle it, plait it – arrange it however you want.

BROTHER AND SISTER

Illustrated on page 13

You will need

Tartan cotton: 2 pieces, each 21 x 21cm/8¼ x 8¼in (blouse/shirt); 2 pieces, each 45 x 3cm/17¾ x 1¼in (collar); 2 pieces, each 80 x 15cm/31½ x 6in (skirt/pants). **Red felt:** 22 x 22cm/8½ x 8½in (jacket). **Bias binding:** 1m/3ft. Elastic. **White jersey:** 2 pieces, each 14 x 6cm/5½ x 2½in (socks). **Black felt:** 4 pieces, each 9 x 7cm/3½ x 2¾in (shoes).

The girl's skipping rope is made from fine cord with wooden beads for the handles.

See page 8 for instructions on making the shoes and socks.

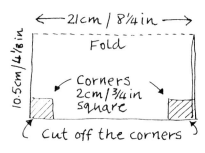

Blouse / Shirt

←— 21cm / 8¼in —→

10.5cm / 4⅛in

Fold

Corners 2cm / ¾in square

Cut off the corners

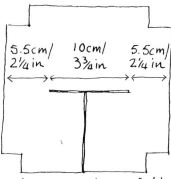

| 5.5cm / 2¼in | 10cm / 3¾in | 5.5cm / 2¼in |

Cut an opening up the centre front and for the neck

Collar

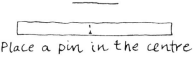

Place a pin in the centre

Oversew 1 long edge
Run gathering stitches along the other

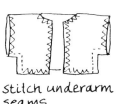

stitch underarm seams
oversew all raw edges

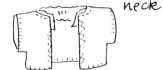

Stitch collar around neck opening, easing to fit

Turn back the collar
Close with a button & loop or 2 pieces of Velcro

Jacket
Fold at shoulder

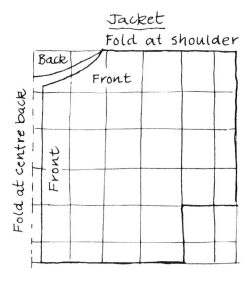

Back

Front

Fold at centre back

Front

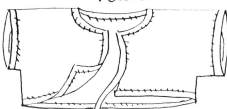

Stitch under the arms
Turn to right side
Stitch bias binding around all raw edges

11

The Skirt and the Pants

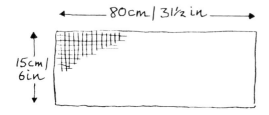

Turn down a hem along one of the long sides

Stitch together the two short sides

Skirt

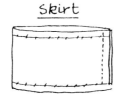

Turn up a hem along the other long edge

Thread elastic through the waistband

Turn to the right side

Pants

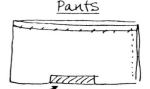

Cut out a little rectangle (6 x 2cm / 2½ × ¾in)

Stitch along the gusset

Turn up hems around both legs

Thread elastic through the top and leg hems

Turn to the right side

LITTLE RED RIDING HOOD

Illustrated on page 16

You will need

Red and white striped jersey (legs). Red and white checked cotton: 2 pieces, each 34 x 28cm/13¼ x 11in (bodice); 2 pieces, each 16 x 8cm/6½ x 3¼in (sleeves). Red cotton: 110 x 13cm/43½ x 5¼in (skirt). Elastic: 22cm/8½in. Red taffeta: 2 pieces, each 20 x 14cm/8 x 5½in (hood); 1 piece 50 x 5cm/20 x 2in (collar). Yellow ribbon: about 50 x 6cm/ 20 x 2½in. White cotton: 10 x 8cm/3¾ x 3¼in (apron). White lace: 30cm/12in. Patterned braid: 60cm/24in. Yellow cotton: 4 pieces, each 8 x 6cm/3¼ x 2½in (shoes). Yellow felt: 2 pieces, each 4 x 2cm/1½ x ¾in (bows).

Legs
Make fron
red and
white
striped
jersey

Shoes
4 identical
pieces (see p.
add a bow f
each

The Blouse

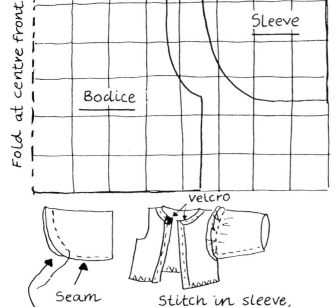

Fold at centre front

Centre

Sleeve

Bodice

velcro

Seam

Gathering stitches

Stitch in sleeve, easing to fit and clipping to seam

Oversew

Stitch the side and shoulder seams
Press down and hem neck and front opening
Oversew the bottom edge

Turn up hems at the bottom of the sleeves
Thread elastic through the cuffs
Turn to the right side

The Skirt

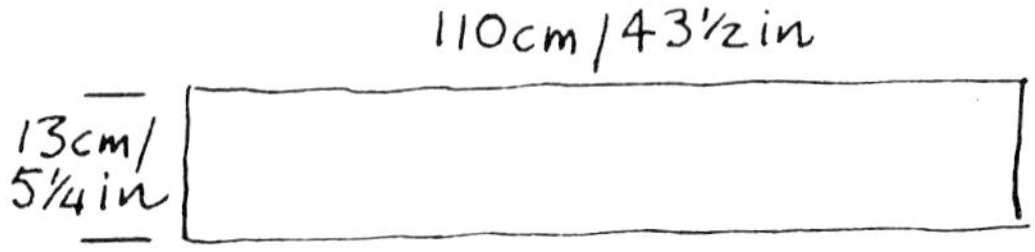

110cm / 43½in

13cm / 5¼in

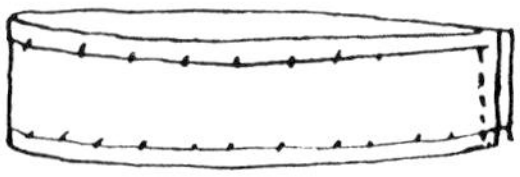

Turn up hems along both long edges
Join the two short sides

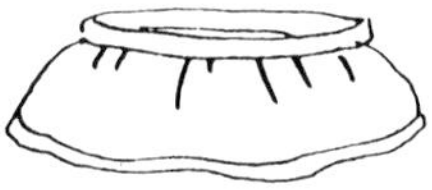

Thread elastic through the top hem
Turn to the right side

The Hood

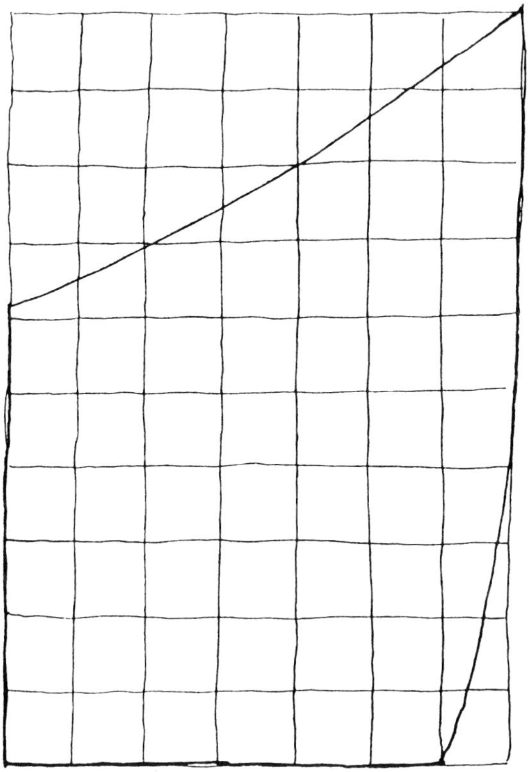

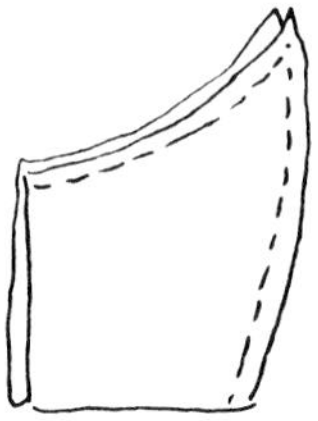

Stitch with right sides together

Turn back the front edge by about 1cm / ½in

Cut off the top angle

Turn to the right side

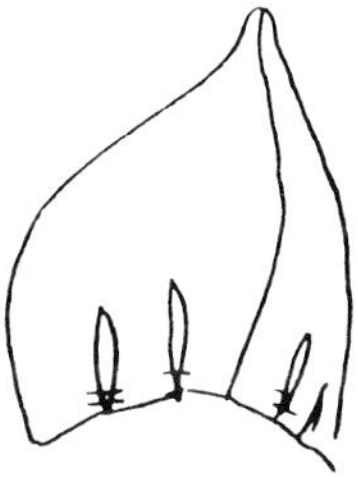

Make 2 darts each side of the back seam

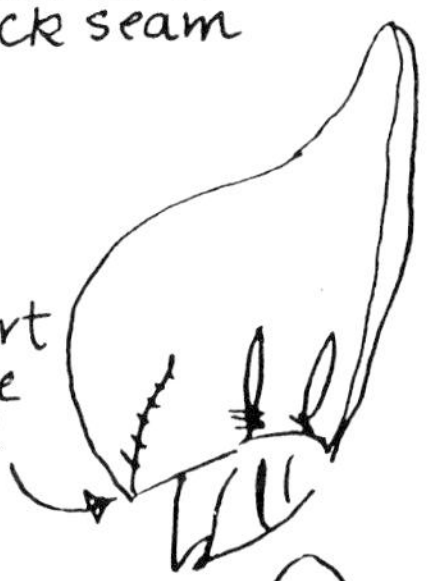

Make a dart at each side of the front

The Collar

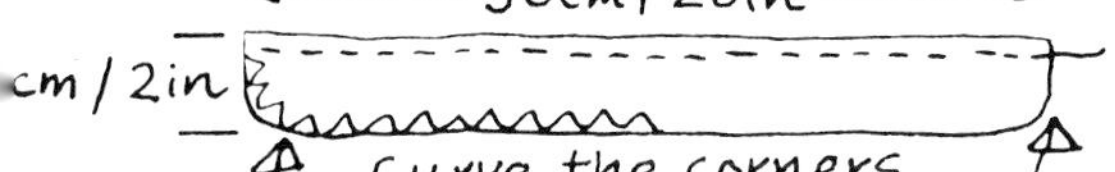

50cm / 20in

cm / 2in

Curve the corners

oversew edge   gather other edge

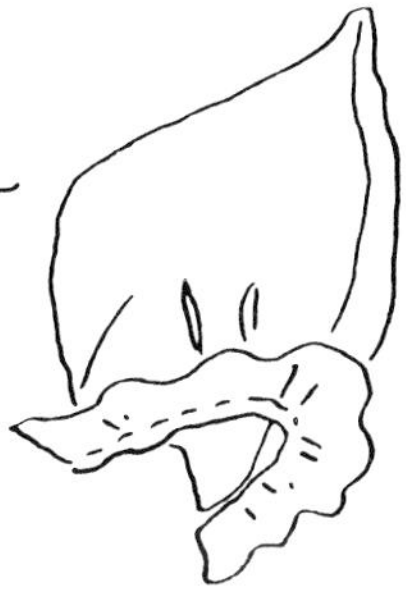

Tie with ribbon

The apron

Stitch lace to 3 sides

Gather the top edge

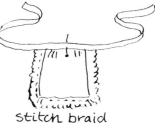

stitch braid along top edge

The basket

Crochet 2 stitches

Work 6 stitches into the first stitch

Continue to work in circles, making 2 stitches every 6 stitches

Fasten off after 5-6 rows

Wind wool around a piece of card 10 × 1cm / 3¾ × ½ in

Stitch handle in place

THE FAIRY

Illustrated on page 19

You will need

Pink cotton: 1 piece 60 x 18cm/24 x 7in (skirt); 2 pieces, each 12 x 9cm/4³/₄ x 3¹/₂in (sleeves); 4 pieces, each 10 x 7cm/3³/₄ x 2³/₄in (shoes).

Pink net with silver spots: 1 piece 60 x 18cm/24 x 7in (stitched over skirt); 2 pieces, each 24 x 9cm/9¹/₂ x 3¹/₂in (oversleeves); 1 piece 20 x 2cm/8 x ³/₄in (headdress).

Blue cotton: 1 piece 75 x 5cm/30 x 2in (frill around skirt); 2 pieces, each 14 x 11cm/5¹/₂ x 4¹/₂in (bodice); 1 piece 22 x 15cm/8¹/₂ x 6in (headdress).

Blue net with silver spots: 1 piece 75 x 5cm/30 x 2in (stitched over skirt frill);1 piece 45 x 3cm/17³/₄ x 1¹/₄in (ruff); 2 pieces, each 22 x 3cm/8¹/₂ x 1¹/₄in (frill around wrists); 1 piece 22 x 15cm/8¹/₂ x 6in (stitched over headdress).

Silver braid: 1 piece 54cm/21¹/₄in (skirt); 2 pieces, each 12cm/4³/₄in (cuffs); 27cm/10¹/₂in (headdress).

Pink ribbon: 50cm/20in (belt). **Elastic. Lightweight card:** approximately 22 x 15cm/8¹/₂ x 6in. **Wooden dowel:** 15 x 0.5cm/6 x ¹/₄in. **Blue and pink tissue paper. Silver star.**

Cut out the bodice from the template on page 20

Stitch the shoulder and side seams

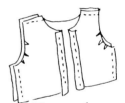

Turn down the back opening

Run gathering stitches along one side of the ruff

Gather the ruff and stitch it to the bodice

Stitch the sleeve seams

Turn up the cuffs

Stitch the short seam of net for the oversleeves
Gather along the other ends

Turn to right
Gather the ends
Gather one side of the ruff.

Turn the bodice right side out
Slip on the oversleeves
Stitch into position

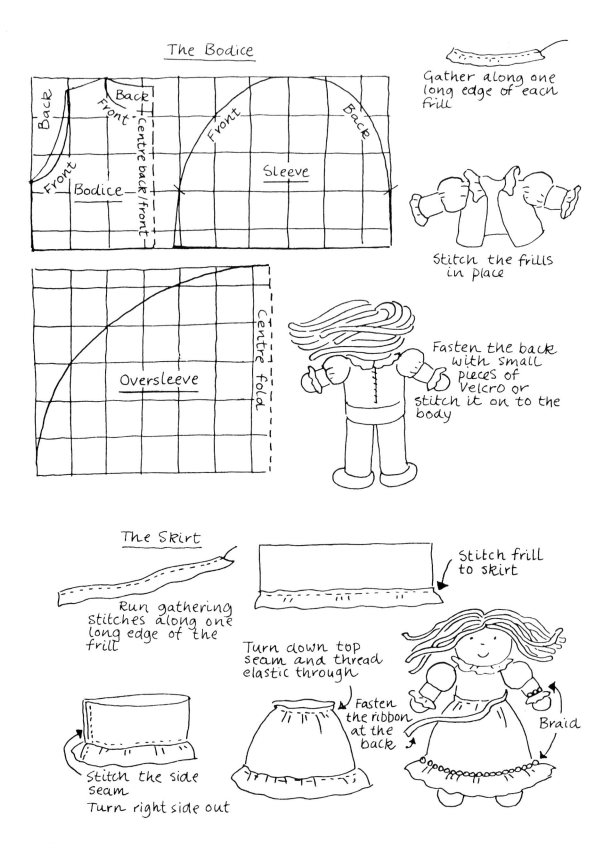

The Bodice

Back
Back
Front
Front
Centre back/front
Front
Sleeve
Bodice
Back

Oversleeve
Centre fold

Gather along one long edge of each frill

Stitch the frills in place

Fasten the back with small pieces of Velcro or stitch it on to the body

The Skirt

Run gathering stitches along one long edge of the frill

Stitch frill to skirt

Turn down top seam and thread elastic through

Fasten the ribbon at the back

Braid

Stitch the side seam
Turn right side out

The Headdress

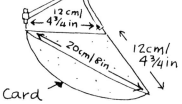

12 cm/ 4¾ in

20cm/8in

12cm/ 4¾ in

Card

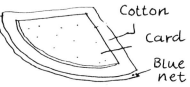

Cotton

card

Blue net

GLUE

Glue fabric edges to the card

GLUE

Glue braid around the bottom edge

Fasten pink net to the top

The Magic Wand

Tissue paper

GLUE

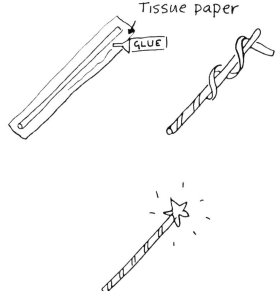

THE PRINCESS

Illustrated on page 23

You will need

White and gold lamé: 1 piece 60 x 24cm/24 x 9½in (skirt); 1 piece 110 x 8cm/43½ x 3¼in (skirt frill). **Red lamé:** 1 piece 70 x 20cm/27½ x 8in (overskirt). **Silver lamé:** 2 pieces, each 14 x 10cm/5½ x 3¾in (bodice). **White lamé:** 2 pieces, each 20 x 17cm/8 x 6¾in (sleeves); 1 piece 40 x 8cm/16 x 3¼in (ruff). **Gold braid:** 110cm/43½in, plus sufficient to trim crown. **Lightweight card:** 27 x 8cm/10½ x 3¼in. **Silver paper:** 30 x 16cm/12 x 6½in. **Red ribbon** (bows). **Pearl beads and sequins** (jewellery).

The Bodice

Cut out, using the template on p 24

Stitch the shoulder and side seams

Cut open the centre back
Turn down the neck edge

stitch the under-arm seam
gather the top edge

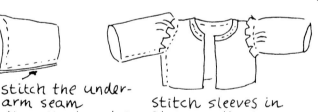

Stitch sleeves in place, gathering to fit

Stitch the bodice onto the doll's body

Turn back the cuff

Gather the cuff around the wrist

Stitch braid over gathers

Fold ruff in two, gather the long open edge

Stitch the gathered ruff in place around the doll's neck

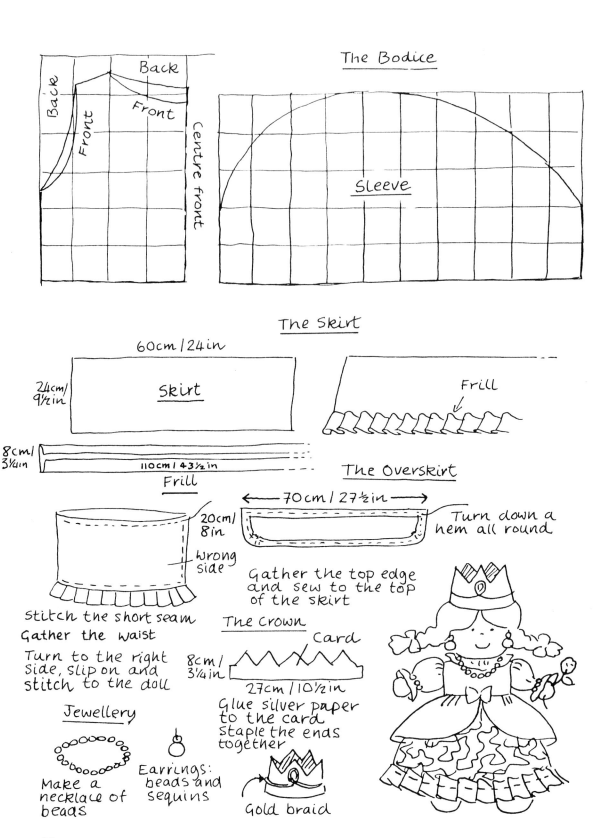

The Bodice

Back

Back

Front

Front

Front

centre front

Sleeve

The Skirt

60cm / 24in

24cm/
9½in

Skirt

Frill

8cm/
3¼in

110cm / 43½in

Frill

The Overskirt

20cm/
8in

70cm / 27½in

Turn down a
hem all round

wrong
side

Gather the top edge
and sew to the top
of the skirt

stitch the short seam
Gather the waist

Turn to the right
side, slip on and
stitch to the doll

The Crown

Card

8cm/
3¼in

27cm / 10½in

Glue silver paper
to the card
Staple the ends
together

Gold braid

Jewellery

Make a
necklace of
beads

Earrings:
beads and
sequins

24

THE WITCH

Illustrated on page 27

Illustrated on page 27

The Hair

Stitch the centre of each strip of felt to the head

You will need

Grey and white striped jersey (legs). **Green felt**: cut into strips 20 x 1.5cm/8 x ½in (hair). **Grey jersey**: 2 pieces, each 26 x 24cm/10¼ x 9½in (bodice); 2 pieces, each 24 x 16cm/9½ x 6¼in (sleeves). **Black and red spotted cotton**: 70 x 17cm/27½ x 6¾in (skirt). **Blue jersey**: 4 pieces, each 12 x 8cm/4¾ x 3¼in (shoes). **Black jersey**: 45 x 44cm/17¾ x 17in (cloak). **Yellow felt** (hat). **Elastic**: shirring and flat. **Black ribbon** (shoes). **Black lace** (hat).

Make the shoes from 4 identical pieces (see p.8)

Grey and white striped jersey for the legs

Stitch a black bow to the shoes

The Bodice

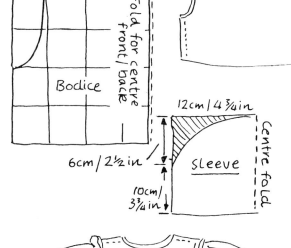

Fold for centre front / back

Bodice

12cm / 4¾in

6cm / 2½in

Sleeve

Centre fold

10cm / 3¼in

Stitch

Gather the top edge

Stitch sleeves to bodice, easing gathers to fit

Stitch narrow hems at neck and cuffs with shirring elastic

The Skirt

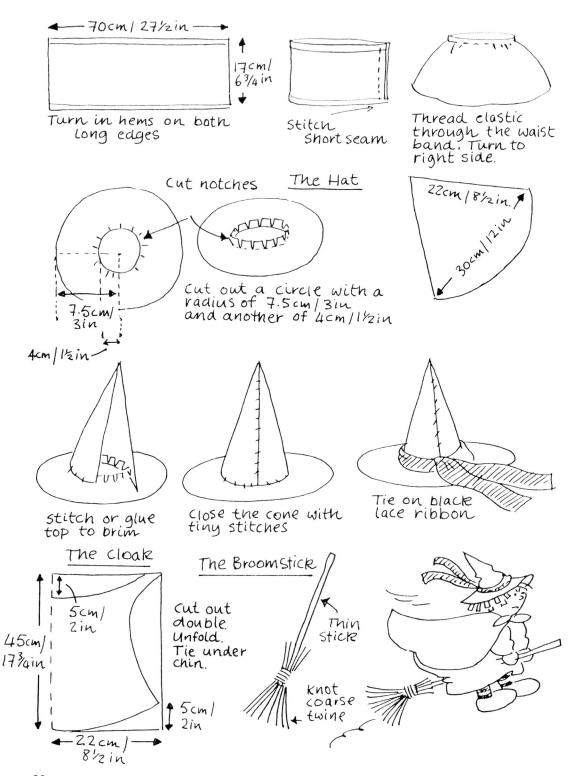

← 70cm / 27½in →

17cm / 6¾in

Turn in hems on both long edges

Stitch short seam

Thread elastic through the waist band. Turn to right side.

Cut notches

The Hat

Cut out a circle with a radius of 7.5cm / 3in and another of 4cm / 1½in

7.5cm / 3in

4cm / 1½in

22cm / 8½in

30cm / 12in

stitch or glue top to brim

Close the cone with tiny stitches

Tie on black lace ribbon

The Cloak

The Broomstick

5cm / 2in

45cm / 17¾in

Cut out double. Unfold. Tie under chin.

5cm / 2in

22cm / 8½in

Thin stick

knot coarse twine

THE PIXIE

Illustrated on page 31

The Pixie's body is made in a different way from the bodies of the other dolls.

You will need

White jersey: 2 pieces, each 22 x 12cm/8½ x 4¾in (head and body); 2 pieces, each 10 x 10cm/3¾ x 3¾in (arms); 2 pieces, each 12 x 7cm/4¾ x 2¾in (upper legs); 2 pieces, each 12 x 4cm/4¾ x 1½in (lower legs). **Petersham:** 16 x 2cm/6½ x ¾in. **Blue and white/pink and white cotton:** 2 pieces, each 24 x 17cm/9½ x 6¾in (trousers); 1 piece 25 x 10cm/10 x 3¾in (bodice); 2 pieces, each 14 x 10cm/5½ x 3¾in (sleeves). **Blue/pink cotton:** 1 piece 42 x 4cm/16½ x 1½in (ruff); 2 pieces, each 15 x 2cm/6 x ¾in (cuff frills); 4 pieces, each 12 x 8cm/4¾ x 3¼in (shoes); 2 pieces, each 24 x 15cm/9½ x 6in (hat). **Elastic.**

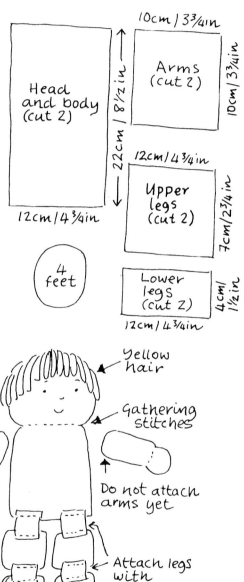

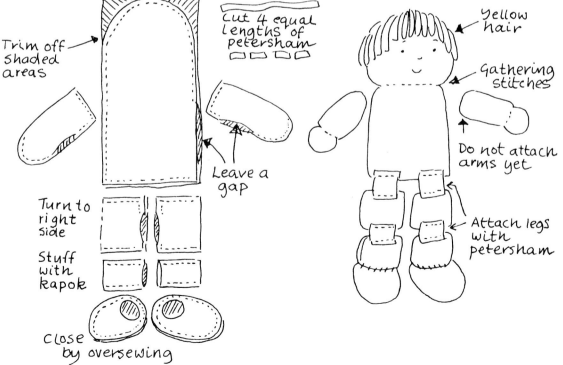

28

The Bodice

Cover the chest with cotton fabric

Stitch the back seam to the doll's body

Run gathering stitches along the ruff

Stitch the gathered ruff around the neck to the top of the bodice

The Sleeve

½ Sleeve

Centre fold

Stitch the frill to the bottom edge

Stitch the underarm seam

Turn to the right side

Run gathering stitches around the top edge

Gather the cuff, above the frill

Place the arm in the sleeve

Stitch sleeve to arm

Attach the sleeves directly to the doll's chest without stitching through the arms

The Trousers

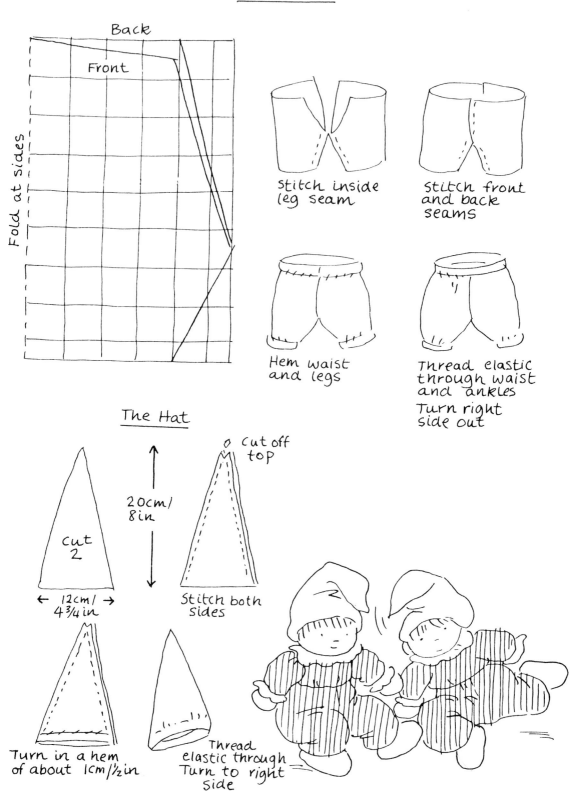

Back

Front

Fold at sides

stitch inside
leg seam

stitch front
and back
seams

Hem waist
and legs

Thread elastic
through waist
and ankles
Turn right
side out

The Hat

cut
2

← 12cm/
4¾in →

20cm/
8in

o cut off
top

Stitch both
sides

Turn in a hem
of about 1cm/½in

Thread
elastic through
Turn to right
side

THE ARTIST

Illustrated on page 33

You will need

Grey jersey: 1 piece 20 x 19cm/8 x 7½in (trousers). **Yellow jersey**: 1 piece 25 x 14cm/10 x 5½in (jacket); 2 pieces, each 13 x 7cm/5¼ x 2¾in (socks). **Blue and yellow jersey**: 1 piece 22 x 12cm/8½ x 4¾in (T-shirt). **Blue felt** (beret). **Black felt**: 4 pieces, each 8 x 5cm/3¼ x 2in (shoes); 1 piece 15 x 7cm/ 6 x 2¾in (satchel). **Elastic. Black ribbon**: 28cm/11in (satchel strap). **Large button. Lightweight card**: 12 x 10cm/4¾ x 3¾in (portfolio). **Black tape** (portfolio ties).

The Beret

Hem the edge and thread elastic through

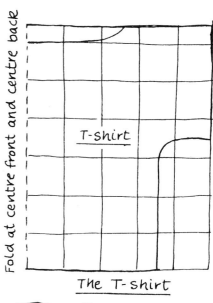

Try on for size before fastening off

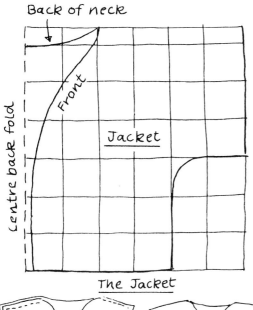

The Jacket

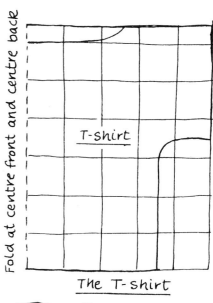

The T-shirt

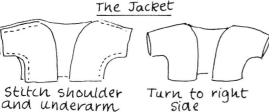

stitch shoulder and underarm seams

Turn to right side

stitch shoulder and underarm seams

Turn to the right side

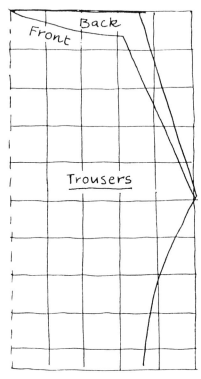

Front

Back

Trousers

stitch inside
leg seams

Stitch front
and back seams

Run two parallel
lines of stitches
around waistline
Thread elastic
through

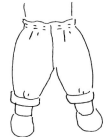

Turn to the right
side. Turn up
bottoms of the
trouser legs once
or twice

The Portfolio

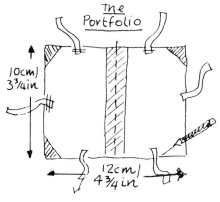

10cm/
3¾in

12cm/
4¾in

Fold the card in half

Colour the corners and
a centre stripe in black

Decorate the rest in green
and black

Stitch or glue tape
in position

The Satchel

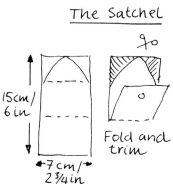

15cm/
6in

7cm/
2¾in

Fold and
trim

Stitch
sides
together

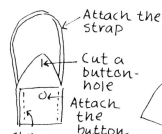

Attach the
strap

Cut a
button-
hole

Attach
the
button

THE HITCH-HIKER

Illustrated on page 37

You will need

White and black check cotton: 2 pieces, each 30 x 16cm/ 12 x 6½in (shirt). **Denim:** 1 piece 20 x 19cm/8 x 7½in (trousers). **Red felt:** 1 piece 20 x 9cm/8 x 3½in (jacket); 1 piece, 15 x 8cm/6 x 3¼in (cap). **Green felt:** 2 pieces, each 14 x 9cm/5½ x 3½in (jacket); 2 pieces, each 9 x 7.5cm/ 3½ x 3in, plus a strip, 20cm/8in (cap). **Blue jersey edging strip:** 60cm/24in (jacket). **Yellow felt:** 2 pieces, each 22 x 2cm/ 8½ x ¾in (jacket). **Blue felt:** 2 pieces, each 13 x 5cm/5¼ x 2in (cap). **Card:** 9 x 7.5cm/3½ x 3in. **Yellow and black dotted cotton:** 1 piece 42 x 14cm/16½ x 5¼in (scarf). **Yellow cotton:** 1 piece 11 x 3.5cm/4½ x 1¼in; 2 pieces, each 22 x 4cm/ 8½ x 1½in; 1 piece 25 x 5cm/10 x 2in (knapsack). **White felt:** 4 pieces, each 8 x 5cm/3¼ x 2in. **Red and blue bias binding or felt** (trainers). **Shirring elastic.**

The Trousers: Make them in the same way as for the Artist (P.34)

The Shirt

Back
Centre back and front
Front
9.5cm/ 3¾in
4.5cm/ 1¾in
Notches 5cm/ 2in

stitch shoulder and underarm seams

Turn down the hem around the neck and cuffs
Thread through shirring elastic

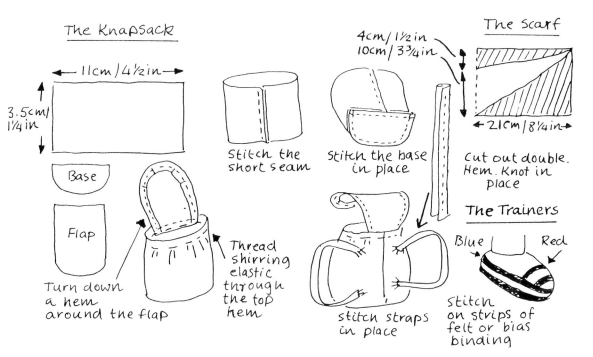

The Knapsack

11cm/4½in
3.5cm/ 1¼in

Base
Flap

Turn down a hem around the flap

Stitch the short seam

Stitch the base in place

Thread shirring elastic through the top hem

stitch straps in place

4cm/1½in
10cm/3¾in

The Scarf

21cm/8¼in

Cut out double. Hem. Knot in place

The Trainers

Blue   Red

stitch on strips of felt or bias binding

The Jacket

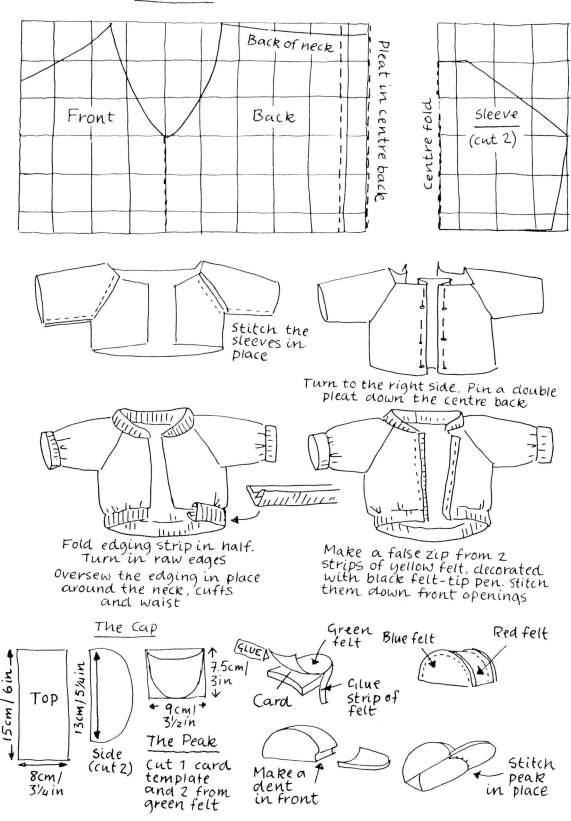

Front

Back of neck

Back

Pleat in centre back

centre fold

sleeve (cut 2)

Stitch the sleeves in place

Turn to the right side. Pin a double pleat down the centre back

Fold edging strip in half. Turn in raw edges
Oversew the edging in place around the neck, cuffs and waist

Make a false zip from 2 strips of yellow felt, decorated with black felt-tip pen. Stitch them down front openings

The Cap

15cm / 6in

Top

8cm / 3¼in

13cm / 5¼in

Side (cut 2)

7.5cm / 3in

9cm / 3½in

The Peak

Cut 1 card template and 2 from green felt

GLUE

Green felt

Card

Glue strip of felt

Blue felt

Red felt

Make a dent in front

Stitch peak in place

THE FOOTBALLER

Illustrated on page 9

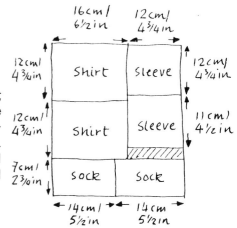

Direction of stripes ⟵ ⟶

16cm/ 6½in — Shirt (12cm/4¾in), 12cm/4¾in — Sleeve (12cm/4¾in)

12cm/4¾in — Shirt, Sleeve 11cm/4½in

7cm/2⅜in — Sock, Sock

14cm/5½in, 14cm/5½in

You will need

Red and green jersey: 1 piece 29 x 24cm/11½ x 9½in (shirt); 1 piece 28 x 7cm/11 x 2¾in (socks). Red cotton: 1 piece 24 x 5cm/9½ x 2in (collar); 1 piece 6 x 5cm/2½ x 2in (button-hole band); 2 pieces, each 26 x 13cm/10¼ x 5¼in (shorts). Black felt: 1 piece 30 x 11cm/12 x 4½in (boots). 3 small buttons. Strips of felt or ribbon: 40cm/16in (laces). Small football.

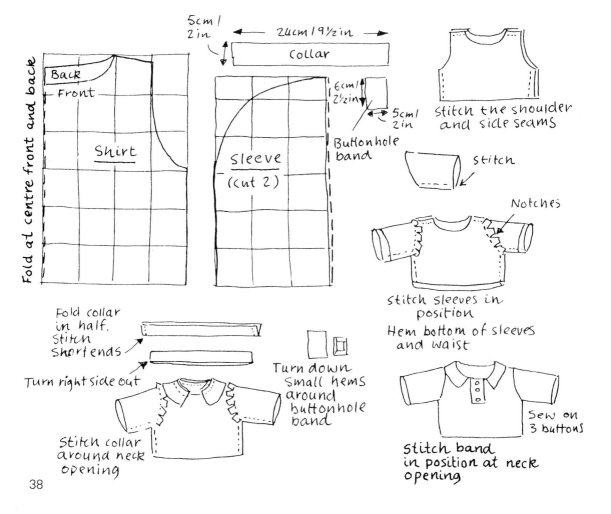

5cm/2in

24cm/9½in

Collar

Fold at centre front and back

Back

Front

Shirt

Sleeve (cut 2)

6cm/2½in

5cm/2in

Buttonhole band

Stitch the shoulder and side seams

stitch

Notches

stitch sleeves in position

Hem bottom of sleeves and waist

Fold collar in half. Stitch short ends

Turn right side out

Stitch collar around neck opening

Turn down small hems around buttonhole band

Sew on 3 buttons

stitch band in position at neck opening

The Shorts

Back

Front

Shorts

Fold at sides

Stitch the inside leg seams

Stitch the front and back seams

Turn down hems at waist and bottom of legs

Thread elastic through the waistband

The Boots

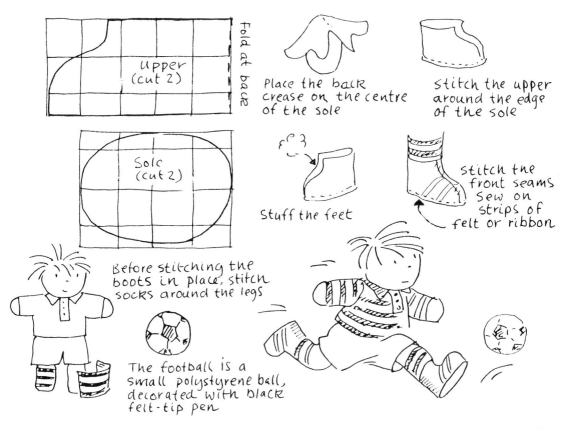

Upper (cut 2)

Fold at back

Sole (cut 2)

Place the back crease on the centre of the sole

Stitch the upper around the edge of the sole

Stuff the feet

Stitch the front seams Sew on strips of felt or ribbon

Before stitching the boots in place, stitch socks around the legs

The football is a small polystyrene ball, decorated with black felt-tip pen

SUPERMAN

Illustrated on page 41

The body of Superman is made in a different way from the bodies of the other dolls.

You will need

White jersey: 2 pieces, each 14 x 12cm/5½ x 4¾in (head); 2 pieces, each 11 x 4cm/4½ x 1½in (hands). **Red jersey:** 2 pieces, each 15 x 14cm/6 x 5½in (body); 4 pieces, each 10 x 6cm/3¾ x 2½in (legs). **Blue jersey:** 2 pieces, each 11 x 9cm/4½ x 3½in (arms); 2 pieces, each 14 x 7cm/5½ x 2¾in (shorts). **Silver lamé:** 4 pieces, each 10 x 10cm/3¾ x 3¾in (boots); 1 piece 38 x 38cm/15 x 15in (cape). **Yellow felt:** 1 piece 28 x 2cm/11 x ¾in (belt); 1 piece 5 x 5cm/2 x 2in (badge).

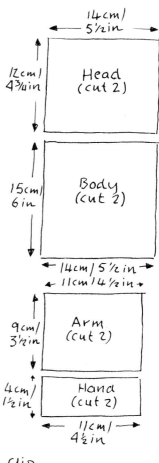

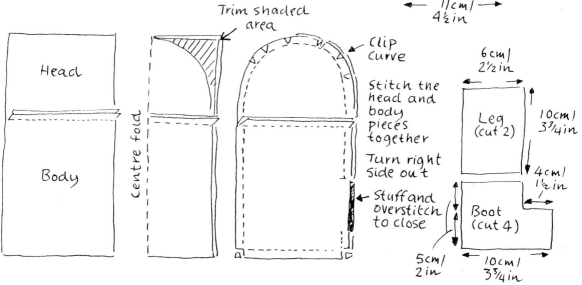

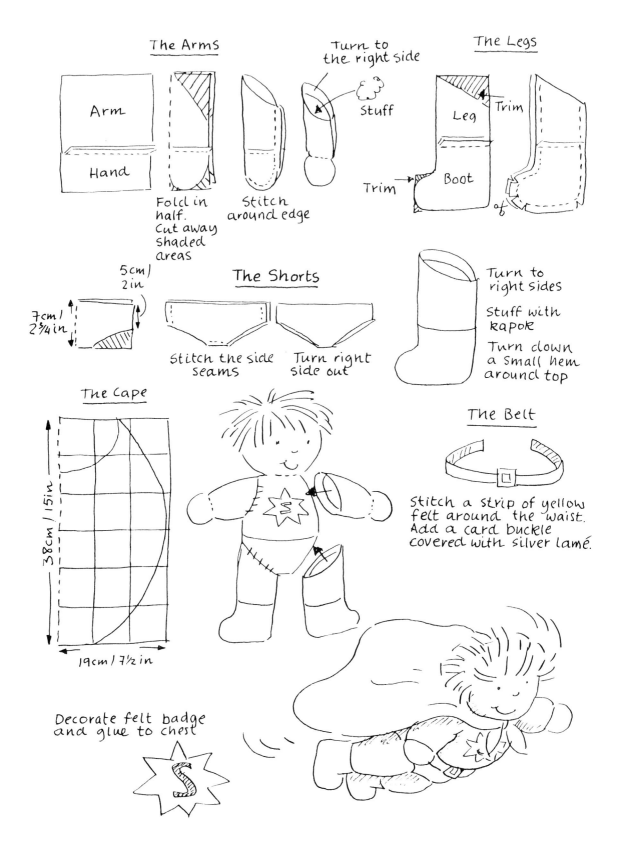

The Arms

Arm

Hand

Fold in half. Cut away shaded areas

Stitch around edge

Turn to the right side

Stuff

The Legs

Leg

Boot

Trim

Trim

of

5cm / 2in

7cm / 2¾in

Turn to right sides

Stuff with kapok

Turn down a small hem around top

The Shorts

Stitch the side seams

Turn right side out

The Cape

38cm / 15in

19cm / 7½in

The Belt

Stitch a strip of yellow felt around the waist. Add a card buckle covered with silver lamé.

Decorate felt badge and glue to chest

S

THE CHEF

Illustrated on page 45

You will need

White cotton: 1 piece 45 x 30cm/17³/₄ x 12in (jacket); 1 piece 48 x 24cm/19 x 9¹/₂in (trousers); 1 piece 34 x 20cm/13¹/₄ x 8in (apron); 1 piece 32 x 14cm/12¹/₂ x 5¹/₂in and 1 circle 16cm/6¹/₂in in diameter (hat); 1 piece 48 x 20cm/19 x 8in (scarf). **White ribbon** (apron ties). **Elastic.**

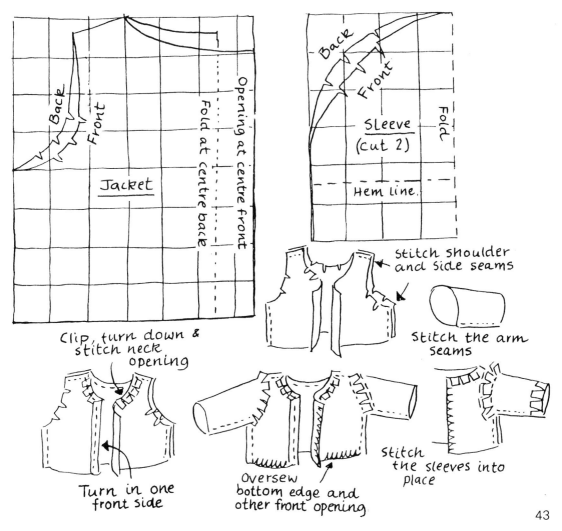

Back Front

Jacket

Fold at centre back

Opening at centre front

Back Front

Sleeve (cut 2)

Fold

Hem line.

Stitch shoulder and side seams

Stitch the arm seams

Clip, turn down & stitch neck opening

Turn in one front side

Oversew bottom edge and other front opening

Stitch the sleeves into place

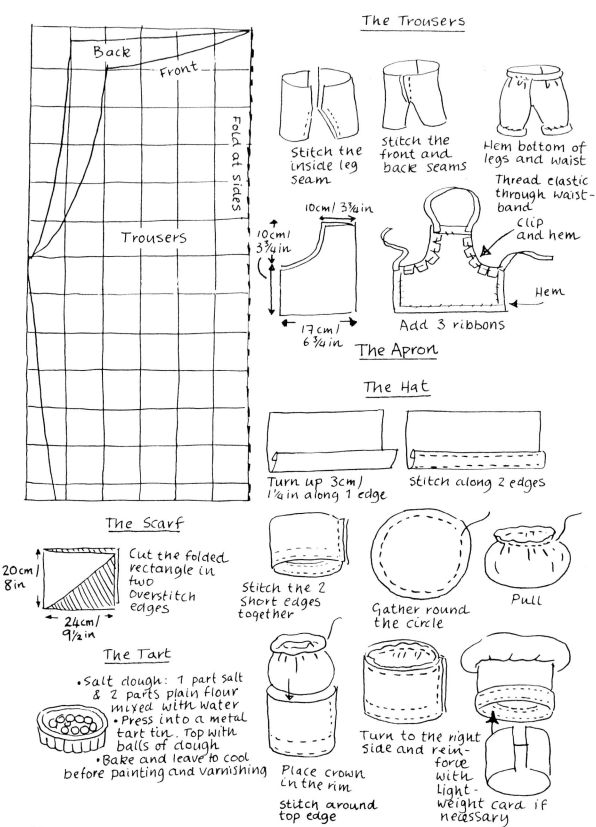

Back

Front

Fold at sides

Trousers

The Trousers

Stitch the inside leg seam

stitch the front and back seams

Hem bottom of legs and waist

Thread elastic through waist-band

10cm / 3¾in

10cm / 3¾in

17cm / 6¾in

Clip and hem

Hem

Add 3 ribbons

The Apron

The Hat

Turn up 3cm / 1¼in along 1 edge

stitch along 2 edges

The Scarf

20cm / 8in

24cm / 9½in

Cut the folded rectangle in two
Overstitch edges

Stitch the 2 Short edges together

Gather round the circle

Pull

The Tart

• Salt dough: 1 part salt & 2 parts plain flour mixed with water
• Press into a metal tart tin. Top with balls of dough
• Bake and leave to cool before painting and varnishing

Place crown in the rim

stitch around top edge

Turn to the right side and rein-force with light-weight card if necessary

LITTLE MISCHIEF

Illustrated on page 5

This doll's body is made in a different way from those of the other dolls. It also has two faces – one happy, one sad – and the hair is, therefore, attached not to the head but to the hat, so that you can choose which face you see.

You will need

Pale pink felt (hands). **Yellow jersey:** 1 piece 30 x 26cm/ 12 x 10¼in (hat); 2 pieces, each 20 x 15cm/8 x 6in (sleeves). **Red jersey:** 1 piece 19 x 8cm/7½ x 3¼in (top); 2 pieces, each 10 x 10cm/3¾ x 3¾in (shoes). **Green jersey:** 1 piece 19 x 8cm/7½ x 3¼in (top); 2 pieces, each 10 x 10cm/3¾ x 3¾in (shoes). **Red striped jersey:** 26 x 3cm/10¼ x 1¼in (collar). **Green and white striped jersey:** 46 x 25cm/18 x 10in (trousers). **Red and white striped jersey:** 46 x 25cm/18 x 10in (trousers). **Petersham. Elastic.**

15cm/6in — Sleeve — 10cm/3¾in

10cm/3¾in

Stitch the arm seam

Template for hand

Attach the legs with petersham

Striped jersey
Green jersey
Red jersey

Red jersey   Green jersey

Gather the bottom of the sleeves. Insert the hands and stitch in place

Place the arm in the sleeve. Gather the top of the sleeve

Stitch sleeves to sides of body
Leave arms free

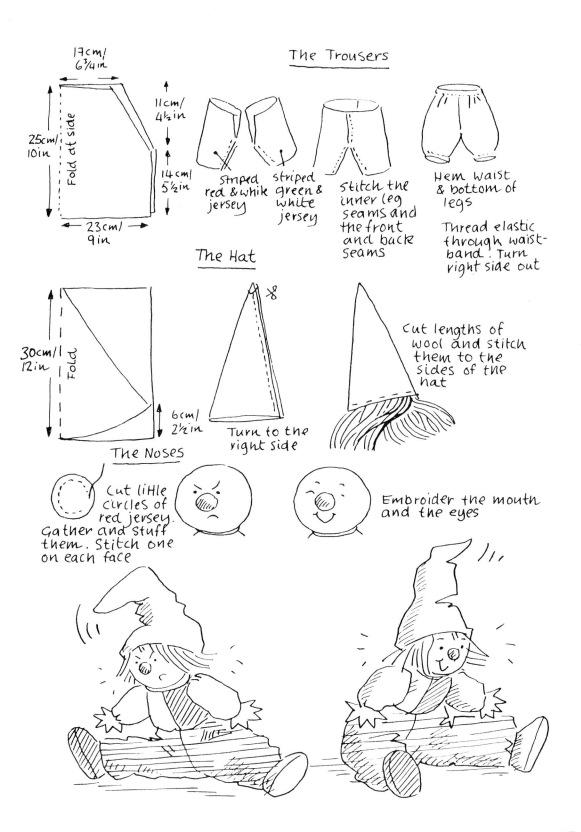

The Trousers

17cm/
6¾in

25cm/
10in

Fold at side

11cm/
4½in

14cm/
5½in

23cm/
9in

striped
red & white
jersey

striped
green &
white
jersey

Stitch the
inner leg
seams and
the front
and back
seams

Hem waist
& bottom of
legs

Thread elastic
through waist-
band. Turn
right side out

The Hat

30cm/
12in

Fold

6cm/
2½in

Turn to the
right side

Cut lengths of
wool and stitch
them to the
sides of the
hat

The Noses

Cut little
circles of
red jersey.
Gather and stuff
them. Stitch one
on each face

Embroider the mouth
and the eyes